To

From

WHAT
I LOVE
ABOUT YOU,
MOM

Mom

. . . .

I wrote this book for you as a way of showing my love and appreciation. I am the person I am today thanks to your love and support.

This book contains some treasured memories of our relationship, and it is an expression of my gratitude to you for being the greatest mom I could ever ask for.

. . . .

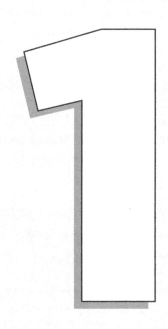

YOU'RE THE BEST
AT MAKING ME FEEL...

2

I'M PROUD THAT YOU'RE MY MOM BECAUSE...

....

....

....

....

....

....

....

....

....

....

....

....

....

3

THERE IS NO ONE
LIKE YOU, WHO CAN...

YOU'VE ALWAYS ENCOURAGED ME TO...

5

I AM THE BEST VERSION OF MYSELF TODAY BECAUSE YOU...

6

I KNOW THAT
I CAN ALWAYS COUNT
ON YOU FOR...

THE QUALITY
I MOST VALUE IN YOU
IS YOUR...

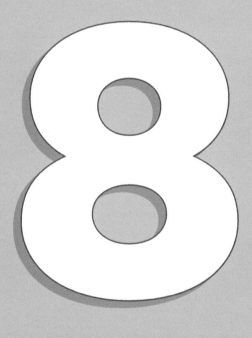

YOU AND I
ARE SIMILAR IN...

SOME
OF MY
FAVORITE
SAYINGS
OF YOURS
ARE...

I WANT YOU
TO KNOW THAT...

....

....

....

....

....

....

....

....

....

....

....

....

....

....

10

MY FAVORITE DAYS TOGETHER ARE WHEN WE...

11

YOU HAVE A WAY OF MAKING PEOPLE FEEL...

12

I'LL NEVER FORGET
THE TIME(S)...

13

WE RESPECT EACH OTHER'S OPINIONS EVEN THOUGH WE DISAGREE ABOUT...

14

I CHERISH OUR BOND BECAUSE...

15

THANK YOU FOR
ALWAYS BEING HONEST
ABOUT...

THESE ARE SOME PLACES I'D LOVE TO VISIT WITH YOU...

16

I'LL FOREVER BE REMINDED OF YOU WHENEVER I...

17

YOU MAKE THE WORLD
A BETTER PLACE
WITH YOUR...

18

YOU SOMEHOW KNOW JUST WHAT (OR WHAT NOT!) TO SAY WHEN...

19

I'LL ALWAYS REMEMBER...

20

THE MOST IMPORTANT LESSON YOU EVER TAUGHT ME WAS TO...

21

YOUR GREATEST
SUPERPOWER IS...

22

IF I COULD GO ON A SPECIAL TRIP WITH YOU, WE WOULD...

THESE ARE SOME OF THE BEST WORDS OR PHRASES TO DESCRIBE YOU...

23

MY MOST CHERISHED MEMORY OF YOU IS WHEN...

24

YOU ALWAYS
MAKE ME LAUGH
WHEN YOU...

25

I WISH I HAD YOUR TALENT FOR...

26

YOU DESERVE
AN AWARD FOR...

27

YOU'LL ALWAYS BE...

28

I'M MOST GRATEFUL
FOR YOUR...

29

THANK YOU
FOR ALWAYS...

30

MOM, YOU ARE...

I LOVE YOU, MOM

IMPORTANT INSTRUCTIONS

Before completing this book, please read our important **How-To Guide.**

Inside the How-To Guide you'll find:
- Suggested ideas for each prompt in the book
- Hints and tips on completing the book

To access the How-To Guide, simply scan the QR code below

Or visit
www.questionsaboutme.com/mom

Made in the USA
Monee, IL
04 April 2025

15092091R00046